Christian Counseling: An Introduction

A concise guide for ministers, and Christian workers in the field of Christian Counseling

Written By:

Craig Lantz

Sophia's House Publications
Lansing, Michigan
USA

Christian Counseling: An Introduction

A concise guide for ministers, and Christian workers in the field of Christian Counseling

Sophia's House Publications
4588 Seaway Dr.
Lansing, Michigan 48911
Telephone: 517-719-5801
Email: craiglantz@live.com

First Printing 2012

ISBN-13: 978-1-4701-3365-8

ISBN-10: 1-4701-3365-2

BISAC: Psychology / Psychotherapy / Counseling

Printed in the United States of America

TABLE OF CONTENTS

PREFACE...III

CHAPTER   PAGE

1. Introduction to Christian Counseling.............................1

2. Psychology and Counseling..9

3. Introduction to Nouthetic Counseling............................18

4. The Practice of Nouthetic Counseling............................29

5. Crises Counseling...39

6. Marriage Counseling...50

7. Psychotherapy and Counseling....................................57

8. Christian Psychiatry..69

9. Conclusion..74

APPENDIX

1. How to counsel the Homosexual...................................76

2. The problem with modern Psychology: Why it doesn't work........78

3. Demon Possession: "The Devil made me do it syndrome"...........80

SELECTED   BIBLIOGRAPHY..82

PREFACE

It needs to be said that the depth of research for this paper is not as deep as it could have been. It is intended to be a short and concise guide to help ministers and Christian workers have an introductory background in the field of <u>Christian Counseling</u>. It is admitted that the treatment of the chapters are, in a sense, superficial. However, the goal of this paper is to cover, in one broad stroke, some of the main issues and topics that are relevant to the reader. If the current reader is interested in reading more about the topics covered in this paper, then, by all means consult the selected bibliography in the back. It is humbling to know that more, much more, could have been said about Christian Counseling. However, for what has been said, I hope that God will get the glory for the originality of the research.

The need for Christian counseling is greater than ever before. We need to be, therefore, more equipped as Christian leaders to serve the body of Christ. To Him be the glory and honor for all of our victories and accomplishments.

Craig Lantz

CHAPTER ONE

INTRODUCTION TO CHRISTIAN COUNSELING

There are many different forms of counseling and therapy. But what we are focusing on in this paper is the concept of Christian Counseling in particular. Moreover, we need to define what Christian Counseling itself is, and how Christianity can be a vital tool in the whole counseling arena. Gary R. Collins, PH.D., clearly defines for us what counseling does, and the role of the Christian counselor. Collins says:

Counseling attempts to provide encouragement and guidance for those who are facing loses, decisions, or disappointments. Counseling can stimulate personality growth and development; help people cope more effectively with the problems of living with inner conflict, and with crippling emotions; assists individuals, family members, and married couples resolve interpersonal tensions or relate effectively to one another; and assist persons whose life patterns are self-defeating and causing unhappiness. The Christian counselor seeks to bring people into a personal relationship with Jesus Christ and to help them find forgiveness and relief from the crippling effects of sin and guilt. Ultimately, the Christian hopes to help others become disciples of Christ and a discipler of others.[1]

Counseling, then, attempts to help people solve their problems in areas of their lives that they are not competent to deal with. As Collins pointed out, the Christian counselor seeks to bring people into a relationship with Christ. People need to understand that many of the problems that they have can be traced back to their Spirituality, or lack of it. They may be carrying guilt from their past that has not yet been dealt with. It is the job of the counselor to help the counselee to recognize these things.

A Christian counselor is one who has the following characteristics and personal commitments:

I. Is a deeply committed spirit-guided servant of the Lord Jesus Christ.

II. Is one who applies their knowledge, skills, training, and God-given abilities, and insights.

III. Is one who is committed to the task of helping others move to personal wholeness, interpersonal competence, mental stability, and spiritual maturity.[2]

Christian counselors, then, are true committed believers, that are committed to helping others, with God's help. "Christian counselors recognize the importance of Christian values and of a

---

[1]Gary R. Collins, PH.D., **Christian Counseling: A Comprehensive Guide**, Rev. Ed., (Dallas, Tx.: Word Publishers, 1988), 16.

[2]Gary R. Collins, gen. ed., **Case Studies in Christian Counseling**, Vol. 28, (Dallas, Tx.: Word Publishers, 1991), 4.

personal relationship with Jesus Christ. No person is forced to accept the Christian ways of thinking; but the counselor is constantly aware of the spiritual needs of the counselee. One purpose of Christian counseling is to deal, at least briefly, with these spiritual issues."[3]

THE ROLE OF THE HOLY SPIRIT IN CHRISTIAN COUNSELING

It must be admitted that the Christian Counselor **must** be a person that is dependent upon the Holy Spirit in the counseling process. Jay E. Adams, a well known Nouthetic Counselor, well says that,

> counseling is the work of the Holy Spirit. Effective counseling cannot be done apart from Him. He is called the paraclete who in Christ's place came to be another counselor of the same sort that Christ had been to his disciples.[4]

In many cases, secular or many so-called Christian counseling services have failed to recognize that the Holy Spirit is able to bring change into peoples lives. Jay Adams warns by saying:

> By-passing the Spirit amounts to the denial of human depravity and the affirmation of man's innate goodness. The need for grace and the atoning work of Christ are both undercut, and the counselee is left instead with the husk of a legalistic

---

[3]Collins, **Case Studies**, 16.

[4]Jay E. Adams, **Competent to Counsel: Introduction to Nouthetic Counseling,** (Grand Rapids, Mi.: Zondervans, 1970), 20.

works-righteousness which will lead ultimately to despair since it divests itself of the life and power of the Spirit.[5]

The Christian counselor has a totally different kind of anthropology than does the secular Psychologist. The humanists believe that man is basically good and, that man just needs to be set-free from the inner conflicts that have resulted from the super-ego and the id. The problem in many cases is that man has a sinful nature, and that sinful nature must be changed by the power of the Holy Spirit. For example, the Holy Spirit sanctifies the believer and will help the counselee develop self-control.

The counselor should use the Scriptures as a tool in addition to the guidance of the Holy Spirit. The relationship between the Holy Spirit and the Scriptures are clear. Adams says:

This fundamental relationship in itself should be decisive for any Christian who carefully thinks through the counseling situation. Counseling without the Scriptures can only be expected to be counseling without the Holy Spirit.[6]

TECHNIQUES OF CHRISTIAN COUNSELING

Christian counselors can use a variety of techniques and therapeutic procedures that are designed to help the counselee.

---

[5]Ibid., 20-21.

[6]Adams, 24.

Collins says that there are four basic techniques that will help the counselee make adjustments: (1) Listening; (2) demonstrating interest in the counselee; (3) attempting to understand; and (4) at least occasionally giving direction.[7] Christian techniques are somewhat different from secular therapeutic techniques because the Christian counselor recognizes that man is a spiritual being. A secular counselor, for example, would never pray with a counselee, read Bible passages, or cast out demons. Collins list eight techniques that can be used in Christian therapy and counseling:

1. Private prayer by the counselor for the counselee, without the counselee present.

2. Encouraging the counselee to get involved in a local church; or in other Christian support groups.

3. Praying with the counselee.

4. Reading Bible passages that pertain to the counselors problem.

5. Sharing Bible truths on forgiveness, lead them to Christ, and grow as disciples.

6. The use of inner healing, and healing of memories.

7. Healing in conjunction to James 5:16 (e.g., the laying on of the hands by the elders and anointing with oil).

8. Personal deliverance of demonic oppression, or possession.[8]

---

[7]Collins, **Case Studies**, 10.

[8]Ibid., 13.

The advantage that the Christian counselor has over the humanist counselors is that these techniques can bring great change and help that modern scientific secular methods do not provide. True Christian counseling can be seen as a three-part ministry. "Basically the counselor performs the following functions: listens to the counselee; helps the counselee gain insight; helps the counselee formulate a specific plan of action."[9]

Clyde M. Narramore (1960), in his textbook on counseling, provides us with seven steps to help produce effective Christian counseling. He says in his **Psychology and Counseling** that the counselor must:

1. Provide a place and atmosphere conducive to uninterrupted discussion.

2. Encourage the counselee to talk and express himself freely.

3. Reflect and restate what the counselee says, thereby encouraging him to clarify his own thoughts and to say more.

4. Do not register surprise at any information which the counselee reveals.

5. Refrain from censoring or judging what the counselee says.

6. Encourage the counselee to suggest and discuss his own possible solutions.

---

[9]Paul D. Meier et al, **Introduction to Psychology and Counseling**, 2nd ed., (Grand Rapids, Mi.: Baker Book House, 1991), 313.

7. Maintain a confidential attitude toward all discussion.[10] Whatever techniques that the Christian counselor uses, they must remember that they are only techniques, such as the ones that Narramore has given us. The more important factor for us to remember is that a Christian counselor's goal should be to direct them back towards the word of God and prayer. When it comes to the spiritual problems of man, Christ and His word give us the answers. The counsel given to counselee's must be Biblical in nature in order to truly help people. Johnston warns by saying:

> But if the counsel given is not truly Biblical, it will not continue to work and the counselee will then be more confused and hurt than ever. And this is exactly where many Christians are today. But it is not because the Bible is insufficient. It is because many Christian counselors rely primarily or exclusively on secular resources, rather than on God's word.[11]

As a result of many Christian counselors failing to use God's word as the primary tool to help people, many people have turned to modern Psychology for the answers to life.

I am willing to give some credit to modern secular psychology for giving us some of the answers; but modern psychology fails to recognize that man is spiritual in nature (see Appendix two), and

---

[10]Clyde M. Narramore, **The Psychology of Counseling**, (Grand Rapids, Mi.: Zondervans, 1960), 57.

[11]J. Kirk Johnston, **When Counseling is not Enough: Biblical answers for those who still struggle**, (Grand Rapids, Mi.: Discovery House, 1994), 51.

that many, or even to say that most of man's problems can be traced back to his/her fallen Adamic state, and broken relationship with God his creator.

CHAPTER TWO

PSYCHOLOGY AND COUNSELING

Psychology is one of the most controversial studies of the human behavior in our culture. It will be important to look at in this chapter, what the exact nature of psychology is; we will look at modern psychology, and Christianties version of psychology. We need to extract the good methods and techniques of modern psychology and see how that relates to the benefit of the Christian methods in counseling.

DEFINITION OF PSYCHOLOGY

Psychology can be defined as "The scientific study of the behavior and thinking organisms. Psychology might be thought of as the study of how living creatures interact with their environment and each other, and how they cope with that environment."[1]

In our complicated culture, it can be easy to see that there may be, in fact, a greater need to have a better understanding of how people cope with their environment. Many people are not able to cope well at all with the society in which they live. Psychology has attempted to provide answers to these types of

---

[1]Meier et al, **Introduction to Psychology and Counseling**, 17.

problems.

The purpose of this chapter is not to look at every area of psychology as such, or to analyze its methods; but to see how psychology can relate to theology and counseling. In the church today there is a great tension between the two extremes: all psychology or no psychology and all Bible. "As a result of these tensions, the Christian community has often been suspicious of or even hostile towards psychology and the social sciences."[2]

PSYCHOLOGY AND THEOLOGY

There are four ways of relating psychology and theology together: (1) The first position is the Christianity against psychology position; (2) psychology against Christianity; (3) Christianity and psychology that are two disciplines or ways of finding the truth; and (4) psychology integrates Christianities view of truth.[3] None of these models may stand alone as the best, however, "we as Christians should make use of those psychological concepts that are useful and compatible with Scripture and leave behind those that conflict with our faith."[4] Now concerning theology and psychology, Meier says that

conflicts between theology and psychology are due either to

---

[2]Ibid., 26.

[3]Ibid., 26-28.

[4]Ibid., 29.

error in Biblical interpretation, error in using the scientific method, or both since both are derived from God's revelation; accurate findings in both will not conflict. All truth is God's truth. We do best, therefore, to adopt an eclectic approach, tentatively accepting those principles that have good research evidence and do not conflict with Biblical data.[5]

What we should do, then, is use the methods that are working in psychology that do not conflict with the Bible. The truth that we find in modern psychology is still, nevertheless, truth that can be applicable to counseling and psychology.

PSYCHOLOGY AS RELIGION

Many people feel that psychology has grown up to be a religion in the place of Christianity. Some authors are deeply hostile to the presuppositions of modern-secular-psychology. As we have already stated in the previous chapter that humanistic answers will not truly change the heart or life of an individual. Some feel that the heart of psychology is focusing in on self, or that self-worship is the end result. Paul C. Vitz wrote a book entitled, **Psychology as Religion: The Cult of Self-Worship**, where he argues against psychology in today's culture. The book is built upon five central premises:

1. Psychology as religion exists, and it exists in strength throughout the United States.

---

[5]Ibid., 30.

2. Psychology as religion can be criticized on many grounds quite independent of religion.

3. Psychology as religion is deeply anti-Christian.

4. Psychology as religion is extensively supported by schools, Universities, and social programs that are funded by taxes collected from millions of Christians. This use of money to support what has become a secular ideology raises grave political and legal issues.

5. Psychology as religion has been for years destroying individuals, families, and communities. But in recent years the destructive logic of this system is beginning to be understood, as more and more people discover the emptiness of self-worship. Christianity is presented with a major historical opportunity to provide meaning and life.[6]

Vitz obviously feels very strongly that psychology is anti-Christian and has done great harm to people with its own proclaimed self-help message. The essential nature of the message it gives does not, in fact, change man's sinful nature-the real crux of the problem. Much of modern psychology is built upon the presuppositions of Sigmond Freud. This philosophy says, essentially, that its not my fault: its somebody else's. My super-ego is troubling my id because my parents shoved their morality down my throat. Jay E. Adams well says:

People no longer consider themselves responsible for what they

---

6Paul C. Vitz, **Psychology as Religion: The Cult of Self-Worship**, 2nd ed., (Grand Rapids, Mi.: Wm B. Eerdmans, 1977), xiii.

12

do wrong. They claim that their problems are **allogenic** (others engendered) rather than **autogenic** (self-engendered). Instead of assuming personal responsibility for their behavior, they blame society. Society is easy to blame since what is everyone's responsibility is no-one's responsibility...Freudian psychoanalysis turns out to be an archeological expedition back into the past which a search is made for others on whom to pin the blame for the patients behavior. The fundamental idea is to find out how others have wronged him.[7]

It is clear that modern psychology finds its answers in freudian techniques of finding out whose to blame. It should be pointed out at this point, that many authors, like Adams, see no place for psychology's answer in the life of a Christian. Jim Owen says:

"Christian" psychology's intentions may be commendable but its methodology and presuppositions upon which it depends are not. The sincerity of an individual's faith or the praise worthiness of his compassionate intentions does not give him the permission to undermine the reality of Jesus Christ and His authority and sufficiency as revealed in His word and ministered to us by the Holy Spirit.[8]

The central motif of Owen's book is that modern psychology places

---

[7]Adams, 6.

[8]Jim Owen, **Christian Psychology's war on God's word: The Victimization of the Believer**, (Santa Barbra, Ca.: Eastgate Publishers, 1993), 21.

the blame on others, and makes the person a victim rather than a guilty sinner who is in need of repentance and salvation. Again, Owen loudly speaks:

> "Christian" psychology speaks of victimization; God speaks of implacable enmity of the wicked toward God. "Christian" psychology speaks of man's painful disappointment and hurts; God speaks of mean-spirited profligates. "Christian" psychology speaks of low self-esteem and the need for appropriate self-love; God speaks of the despicable idolatry of self-worship.[9]

Man is not a victim primarily, rather, man is a free-moral agent that has the choice of whether or not they want to sin. People need to take responsibility for their sin and stop blaming others for the results of it. In some cases, Christian psychology "emphasizes man-as-victim rather than man as a sinner. Such a view radically challenges the Biblical doctrines of man's absolute culpability before the cross, the supremacy of the Holy Spirit in the believer's sanctification, and most importantly the sufficiency and authority of Scripture for the believer."[10] John White expresses his concern about the rise of pop psychology:

> The rise of pop psychology and the human potential movement causes me greater concern than the older disciplines-not only because it has infiltrated modern psychology but because, more

---

[9]Owen, 37.

[10]Ibid., 18.

surprising yet, it has infiltrated the church. One would think that these psychologies were poles apart from evangelicalism and fundamentalism. But, amazingly, large segments of the church have swallowed them whole.[11]

EVALUATING PSYCHOLOGY

It is apparent from theses sources presented that there are authors who see many dangers of modern psychology, and "Christian" psychology for that matter. What we need to know is the answer to this question: **How can psychology help in the counseling process?** Many authors see no use of psychology and that the word of God is enough. Gary R. Collins, PH.D., believes that the discoveries in psychology can be useful in Christian counseling. Collins says that,

> the Bible never claims to be a textbook on counseling. It deals with loneliness, discouragement, marriage problems, grief, parent-child relations, anger, fear, and a host of other counseling situations, but it was never meant to be God's sole revelation about helping people.[12]

Collins continues to support the notion that the findings of psychology can be useful. Here Collins looks at the positive side of psychology:

Our knowledge is far from complete and neither is error-free,

---

[11]John White, **Putting the Soul Back in Psychology**, (ILL.: Intervarsity Press, 1987), 67.

[12]Collins, **Christian Counseling**, 22.

15

but careful psychological research and data analysis have led to a vast reservoir of conclusions that are known to help counselee's and people who want to be effective people helpers. Even those who would dismiss the field of psychology frequently use psychological terms in their writings and psychologically derived techniques in their counseling.[13]

Those who advocate the use of psychology and its techniques in Christian counseling, often defend it through the concept of general revelation. In other words, there is a certain level of truth that is revealed to all men and women (e.g., Romans 1:18-20). The basic idea is that God is the source of all truth that can be found. "God is the ultimate source of truth. Because truth exists in God, his creation can represent only an abstraction of it."[14] We can benefit from the truth that is found in psychology. However, "Discovered truth must always be consistent with, and tested against, the norm of revealed Biblical truth."[15] All truth that is discovered must be judged and measured by the standard of the Scriptures, God's special revelation-His revealed word. "We must build from special revelation a grid of knowledge that will allow us to test whether the scientific models and theoretical constructs presented by scientists are indeed in agreement with God's

---

[13]Ibid., 22.

[14]Meier et al, 32.

[15]Collins, 22.

creation."[16]

Whatever scientific truths that can be found in psychology, must be kept in it's proper perspective: **they are only tools to help the person become closer to Christ. If this is not the goal, then, it is not true Christian counseling.** Collins well says that,

we limit our counseling effectiveness when we pretend that the discoveries of psychology have nothing to contribute to the understanding of problems. We compromise our integrity when we overtly reject psychology but then smuggle its concepts in to our counseling-sometimes naively and without even realizing what we are doing.

Let us, accept the fact that psychology can be of great help to the Christian counselor.[17]

_____

[16]Meier et al, 33.

[17]Collins, 22-23.

CHAPTER THREE

INTRODUCTION TO NOUTHETIC COUNSELING

There are many different methods of counseling today. But as believers in Christ, we must put our focus on the methods and practices of counseling that find their roots in the basis of the Scriptures. All true Christian counseling is biblically based, or, it is not true Christian counseling; rather, it becomes a secular answer to life's problems. Jay E. Adams concurs by saying:

Jesus Christ is at the center of all true Christian counseling. Any counseling which moves Christ from that position of centrality has to the extent that it has done so ceased to be Christian.[1]

According to Adams, then, all true Christian counseling must be based upon Jesus Christ. We find that Christ has given us the word of God as our complete foundation of all truth and reality. The Scriptures do, in fact, have plenty to say about counseling.

NOUTHETIC COUNSELING

The concept of nouthetic counseling comes from two Greek words in the New Testament: **Nouthesis** and **Noutheteo**.[2] It will be

---

[1]Adams, **Competent to Counsel**, 41.

[2]Ibid., 41.

18

necessary to quote at least three passages of Scripture where these Greek words are used to better lay the foundation for nouthetic practices in counseling. Paul says in Colossians 3:16: "Let the word of Christ richly dwell within you, with all wisdom teaching and confronting one another **nouthetically.**" Paul also told the Roman Christians saying, "Concerning you, my brethren, I myself also am convinced that you are full of goodness, filled with all knowledge and able to confront one another **nouthetically**" (Romans 15:14). Paul pictured the Christians in Colossia and Rome confronting one another in love and speaking the truth. Again, Paul says in Colossians 1:28 that we should "proclaim him confronting every man **nouthetically.**"

DEFINITIONS AND PRACTICAL IMPLICATIONS

The exact translation for the Greek word **nouthesis** could mean in English to **admonish, warn,** and **teach.**[3] Adams says emphatically that "no one English word quite conveys the full meaning of **nouthesis.**"[4]

The implication of nouthetic counseling is clear, in that, it involves some form of confrontation with another person with a particular problem or sin. Nouthetic counseling involves teaching, admonishing one another, and even warning another believer due to

---

[3]Ibid., 44.

[4]Ibid., 44.

19

sin in that persons life. Adams elaborates on the concept of nouthetic confrontation. He says:

> Nouthetic confrontation, then, necessarily suggests first of all that there is something wrong with the person who is to be confronted nouthetically. The idea of something wrong, some sin, some obstruction, some problem, some difficulty, some need that has to be acknowledged and dealt with is central. In short, nouthetic confrontation arises out of a condition in the counselee that God wants changed. The fundamental purpose of nouthetic confrontation, then, is to effect personality and behavior change.[5]

So, then, when we are talking about nouthetic counseling, we are talking about counseling that is seeking to change the behavior patterns in people's lives. The proper application of the word of God can bring about true change in the life of a believer. What good is it to go to counseling sessions if your not getting helped effectively? Nouthetic counseling is not giving "pat" answers to people so as to pacify them while they continue in sin and unbelief. The word of God will bring judgement to a matter; it is our measuring rod of truth. The secular world has a big problem in that they have no absolute standards by which to judge something by: it's all relative. A Christian who goes to the secular counselor for help will be like a tractor that is stuck in the mud while its wheels keep on spinning: they won't get helped.

---

[5]Ibid., 45.

THE PURPOSE OF SCRIPTURE IN NOUTHETIC COUNSELING

The Apostle Paul said that "All Scripture is inspired by God and is profitable for teaching, for reproof, for correction, for training in righteousness.." (II Timothy 3:16). Paul makes it clear here that the purpose of Scripture fits in with the practice of nouthetic counseling. In Colossians 1:28 Paul speaks "about confronting every man nouthetically in order that every man might be presented perfect in Christ. One might say that the Scriptures themselves are nouthetically oriented."[6] Adams correctly concludes that,

> The Scriptures then, are useful for the nouthetic purposes of reproving, teaching, correcting men in righteousness. Because this is the classic passage concerning inspiration, its primary purpose has been overlooked. Paul was concerned to discuss not only inspiration but primarily the purpose of the Scriptures. He argued that because they were God-breathed, the Scriptures are useful for nouthetic purposes.[7]

THE GOAL OF NOUTHETIC COUNSELING

Adams believes that **love** is the goal in nouthetic confrontation. In I Timothy 1:5, Paul says: "But the goal of our instruction is love from a pure heart, and a good conscience, and a sincere faith." The Greek word for "instruction" means more than

---

[6]Ibid., 51.

[7]Ibid., 51.

simply instruction; "it is instruction imposed authoritatively. The authority of God is presupposed."[8] The purpose of counseling is to foster love towards God and love towards our neighbor. "God's authoritative instruction through the ministry of His word, spoken publicly (from the pulpit) or privately in counseling, is the Holy Spirits means of producing love in the believer."[9] The goal then of nouthetic counseling is to bring men and women into loving God and conforming their lives to His word.

NOUTHETIC COUNSELING IS AUTHORITATIVE

True nouthetic counseling involves the authoritative use of God's word. In other words, the counselor is making practical application of God's word in the life of the counselee. The authoritative counseling does, however, involve the use of directive, nouthetic techniques. Adams says:

Counseling will seek to reverse those sinful patterns which began in the garden of Eden. When he disobeyed God, his conscience was awakened, and out of fear, sinful man fled, covered himself and tried to hide from God. When confronted by God, finding that he could not successfully avoid him, he resorted to blameshifting and excuses. In antithesis to running and hiding, nouthetic counseling stresses turning to God in repentance. Instead of excuse-making or blameshifting,

---

[8]Ibid., 54.

[9]Ibid., 54.

22

nouthetic counseling advocates the assumption of responsibility and blame, the admission of guilt, the confession of sin, and the seeking of forgiveness in Christ.[10] In short, nouthetic counseling is the direct opposite of secular psychology and counseling. Our secular methods say that its someone else's fault, my parents, etc. However, in nouthetic counseling and techniques, the counselor seeks to get the counselee to recognize sin and confess it, repent and turn to God, rather than make excuses for his or her problem or sin. It is true that many people do not want to take responsibility for their actions, and do not believe that there are real consequences for misbehavior. Adams continues by providing some Old Testament examples of nouthetic confrontations:

The same nouthetic methods were used when God, through Nathan, confronted David and when God, in Christ, confronted Peter after his denial. Christ did not hide in the garden or run from the cross but, open and naked he exposed himself to direct encounter with a God of wrath. He pled no mercy in that hour, and made no excuses. He did not attempt to cover or protect himself, but rather he bore the full brunt of the fury of God in the stead of guilty sinners. Nouthetic counseling rests upon the dynamics of redemption, and reflects this fact at every point. Therefore, its power (as well as its fearful responsibility) stems from the fact that nouthetic

---

[10]Ibid., 55.

23

confrontation utilizes the full authority of God.[11]

There are many other examples of nouthetic confrontation. But the point is that the Scriptures are full of examples of people who were confronted nouthetically. Adams hit on a key point in saying that there is a redemptive element in nouthetic confrontation. At the very heart of this type of Biblical counseling is that of redemption. We want to see people's lives restored back to what God intended for us.

THE PASTORAL NOUTHETIC COUNSELOR

The pastor is also a shepherd and care taker over the flock of God. Psalm 23 depicts the relationship between God (the shepherd) and us (his sheep). The shepherd will watch over the sheep and care for them. "The picture embraces the idea of the shepherd's taking care of tired, weary, worn sheep. They also may be discouraged. A large part of pastoral work consists of reviving sheep. Pastors must know how to take tired, discouraged sheep to restful waters and green pastures. They also must protect their sheep from dangers."[12]

The pastor must see that it is his responsibility to take care of the flock of God. The pastor is a nouthetic minister of the word of God. He will take the responsibility to care for them

---

[11]Ibid., 56.

[12]Ibid., 66.

24

through the ministry of the word and prayer. Adams says that

> a minister, therefore, must consider nouthetic confrontation
> as an essential part of his pastoral responsibility. By
> definition, a pastor (i.e., shepherd) cares for worn, weary,
> discouraged sheep. He sees to it that they find rest. The
> pastor, then, must take up his ministry to men in misery.[13]

A true shepherd will practice nouthetic counseling as a vital part of his pastoral ministry and oversight of the flock of God. The goal of every Christian should be to grow into the image of Christ. To be sure, nouthetic counseling is a means to the process of sanctification. We were created in the image of God, but sin has tainted that image (even in the life of a believer). Adams well says that,

> the goal of counseling is the renewal of that image.
> Concretely this means likeness to Christ, who perfectly imaged
> God as man. The attainment of that goal is achieved as a
> client changes from his former sinful life patterns and grows
> into the stature of Christ (Eph. 4:13).[14]

This process of sanctification, then, means that the image of God in man is being restored to what it was in the life of Adam. In order for this to happen, however, is that it involves change. Modern psychology says that the homosexual, for example, can't change his sexual orientation because, he was born that way. But,

---

[13]Ibid., 67.

[14]Ibid., 74.

25

the Scriptures are clear that people can change, and be changed by the power of the Holy Spirit. People do not have to continue to sin, lust, steal, abuse their children, etc. God says we can stop all of that nonsense "if" we will repent and believe the gospel. A turn-about change in our thinking, actions, and attitudes is possible because, change is possible by the power of God. This is the central issue that humanistic psychology has left out: the power of God, hence, their failure to give the world the true answer. Again, Adams here defends (passionately) the thesis that people can change.

> Personality can be changed. God, throughout history, has turned Jacob's into Israel's, Simons into Peters, and Sauls into Pauls...Nouthetic Counselors regularly see patterns of 30-40 years' duration altered. What was learned can be unlearned. An old dog can learn new tricks...God's word changes their thinking, changes their behavior. Change is an important matter to nouthetic counselors. The Scriptures everywhere anticipate change. The Holy Spirit is the Spirit of change. His activity is everywhere represented as the dynamic and power behind the personality changes in people.[15]

The plain and simple truth is that many people do not want to change. For many, they are afraid of change. But to a Christian, change is of great value. Our life as believers will be of

---

[15]Ibid., 76.

constant change if we are going to be effective witnesses for Christ. We must be a flexible people who must be willing to adopt, change, re-think things, develop new patterns of behavior. In short, "Christians must change in order to become like Christ. Growth means changing into the fullness of the stature of Christ."[16] Adams summarizes the role of the pastor in counseling:

> Fundamentally, then, pastoral counseling is helping Christians to become sanctified. Counseling involves helping people to put off old patterns which grew out of rebellion toward God, and helping them to put on new practices which grow out of obedience to God. This is the shepherd's challenge, opportunity and duty.[17]

CHAPTER SUMMARY

What we said in this chapter is that first, Jesus Christ must be the center of all true Biblical Christian Counseling. Nouthetic Counseling is founded upon two Greek words in the New Testament: **nouthesis and noutheteo.** These words basically mean to **admonish, teach, and warn.** We looked at several Scriptures that have these Greek words in them. We saw that the central idea in nouthetic counseling is that the counselors seeks to use the word of God to bring change in the life of a believer. Nouthetic Counseling is authoritative because, it is rooted in Scripture and Scripture

---

[16]Ibid., 77.

[17]Ibid., 77.

carries true authority. The counselee must accept their responsibility for their actions. This is the essential turning point between secular and Christian counseling. People are responsible. Lastly, we learned that the pastor has a great role as a nouthetic counselor. He is to shepherd the flock of God in a nouthetic fashion. The goal of nouthetic counseling is a means to the process of sanctification in the life of a Christian. And this involves change. We discussed the fact that people can change. You can teach an old dog new tricks. Change, however, is only possible by the power of the Holy Spirit.

CHAPTER FOUR

THE PRACTICE OF NOUTHETIC COUNSELING

In this chapter we will look at some of the philosophical and theological presuppositions of nouthetic counseling, as well as some techniques of the nouthetic counselor that have helped to bring change in the life of the counselee.

Many times Christian Counselors forget the fact that counseling is a Spiritual battle. We are fighting against the unseen forces of darkness. We are called to stand against all the schemes of the Devil, all the temptations of the flesh, and all anti-God philosophies of the this world system. Adams concurs by saying:

> The counselor must consider himself a soldier of christ engaging in spiritual warfare when counseling. For that battle the "full armor of God" alone is sufficient. Unbelieving counselors not only lack such equipment, but, moreover, obviously are totally ignorant of the true nature of this situation. In fact, since they are soldiers in the army of Satan, they are on the other side and, therefore, hardly can be relied upon to free Christian counselees from Satan's

grip.[1]

It is clear that the fundamental presupposition is that the counselor must have a Christian foundation, and, a good understanding of the Spiritual warfare that is taking place in peoples lives. There is a completely different way of relating to counselee's from a Christian point of view. The Christian Counselor recognizes the fact that there is a sin problem. And that in many cases, counselee's are struggling with sin in their lives as a root problem that creates much of the guilt and frustration in peoples lives. In our modern thinking, and secular psychology, people do not see themselves as responsible for their sin, and are even bewildered at sins consequences. Adams strongly says that,

> common themes of sin and the sinful attempts to avoid sin's consequences paint a despicable picture of man. He rejects God, becomes miserable before God because of guilt, runs from God, and then (on top of it all) blames God for his own sin! And so often this is precisely the state in which the counselor first meets the counselee.[2]

The fact is that, nouthetic counselors will have to confront sin in the life of the counselee, and, call a "spade" a "spade."

---

[1]Jay E. Adams, **The Christian Counselor's Manual: The Practice of Nouthetic Counseling**, (Grand Rapids, Mi.: Zondervans, 1973), 117.

[2]Ibid., 124.

People need to take responsibility for their own life and stop blaming other people (in particular their parents) for their miserable state. Again, change is the goal.

EFFECTIVE BIBLICAL CHANGE

The goal in nouthetic counseling is to bring effective and permanent change in the life of the counselee. The fact is, is that people can change: you can change. The past can't be changed, but it can be forgiven and forgotten as Adams says:

> The past can be dealt with only in the present by forgiveness, rectification, reconciliation, and other changes that must be made today. Counselors, then, must not allow themselves to become ensnared by the web of fretting, guilt, self-pity, discouragement, and regrets in which some counselees have become entangled.[3]

The clear task of the counselor is to call people to repentance: a change of mind and heart that will lead people to a new lifestyle. The counselor "must insist that every change that God requires of any Christian is possible. Age is no insuperable hinderance, heredity cannot remove responsibility, and the presence of a well-cultivated life-style is not too formidable for the grace of God. The Scriptures give the needed hope, directions, and goals, the Holy Spirit provides the power, and Christian discipline is the

---

[3]Ibid., 173.

method."[4]

As Christians, we should not fear change. All change that is long lasting will come about as the result of the work of the Holy Spirit. As long as a change is oriented toward something good and godly, then, by all means we should seek change. No single person will ever be able to say, "There is nothing more to learn from God's word, nothing more to put into practice tomorrow, no more skills to develop, no more sins to be dealt with."[5] We must understand, as nouthetic counselors, that change in the life of the counselee will come about as a result of discipline, prayer, repentance, and study of God's word and obeying it. However, this is not the simple solution that many so-called Christians want to hear. Many people would like to believe that they can practice sin and live a backslidden life without consequences. But this is not reality. Yes, change is possible in Jesus Christ, by the power of the Holy Spirit, and by His word.

ASKING THE RIGHT QUESTIONS

It is important to understand that a vital part of counseling is gathering data. We must have all the facts. Asking questions to the counselee is a valid and vital method of gathering data. The three most basic questions that need to be asked are: (1) What

---

[4]Ibid., 174.

[5]Ibid., 184.

is your problem? (2)   What have you done about it? and (3)   what do you want us to do?[6] These questions may seem to be very basic, but, in fact these are the very questions that need to be answered. The counselee should be able to answer these questions that will give the nouthetic counselor a framework out of which they can counsel.

As the counseling session goes on, the counselor must continue to as deeper more probing questions about the subject matter and problem. If the counselee, for example, gives some sort of short and vague answer, then, the counselor should ask more probing questions so that all the ambiguities get cleared up. "Biblical counselors maintain control and guide the session at all times."[7]

DEALING WITH ANGER

In counseling, one of the greatest problems to be dealt with is that of anger in men and women. Of course we understand that God is angry at sin. But what we want to address in this section is how people should deal with anger. Anger is an emotion; if it is not ventilated or controlled properly, it can be extremely damaging. All emotions, however, can become destructive when we fail to express them in harmony with Biblical limitations and structures. Many times, people with "bad tempers" simply blow up

---

[6]Ibid., 274.

[7]Ibid., 289.

and vent their anger towards other people around them.

In some secular counseling circles, they practice ventilation as a means of letting the person blow off steam. In these groups people are allowed to beat up on pillows and dummies of people that they are angry at. However, the Scriptures are clear that this type of anger ventilation is wrong (e.g., Prov. 29:11). There is a righteous way of handling anger so that people do not get hurt. People must learn to release their tension of anger toward the problem rather than at the other person. A person can control their anger much better if they develop a solution-oriented frame of mind rather than a problem-oriented frame of mind. Adams says:

> Solution oriented Christians size up the problem, try to fix the responsibilities, and then turn as quickly as possible toward solving the problem biblically...The energies of emotions will be focused upon the solution to the problem, not upon the problem maker.[8]

We must understand that anger is a powerful emotion that can be used as a motivator to fix the problems we are often facing. The counselor's task, then, is "to teach the counselee God's way of using anger: by directing all of it's energies toward the solution of the issue that has arisen in order to destroy and remove any and all impediments that stand between ourselves and another."[9]

_____

[8]Ibid., 354.

[9]Ibid., 355.

It is possible for Christians to live without anger (unrighteously expressed), bitterness, and wrath. The counselor should help the counselee to develop healthy attitudes that are godly and productive. The counselee must be reminded that Jesus loved the unlovely, ungodly sinners, law breakers, and so too, Christians can learn to love each other just as He loved us. Many times in Christian counseling, the solution will boil down to whether or not the counselee will follow Jesus' example. It is possible to love as Jesus loved. True love, in fact, is not based upon feeling. "Love first can be expressed and learned as giving. That is the cure of love. As the counselee gives, the feeling of love will follow."[10]

A counselee who really loves will be a giver, not a taker by nature. God is a giver. John 3:16 says, "For God so loved the world that He gave his only begotten son..." A giver, or someone who is giving to another in a relationship, will bring about a new dynamic in a relationship that has been dead. "The spirit of giving brings about a new relationship. It provides an atmosphere in which communication may grow and thrive."[11]

HELPING THE DEPRESSED

A person can become depressed for many different reasons. Some people lose their jobs, get divorced, sin, etc. All of these

---

[10]Ibid., 367.

[11]Ibid.

events or experiences are factors that can play a part in depression. But, as Adams says,

> the important fact to remember is that a depression does not result directly from any one of these factors, but rather comes from a cyclical process in which the initial problem is mishandled in such a way that it is enlarged in downward helixical spirals that eventually plunge one into despair.[12]

This downward cycle seems to slowly enslave its victims into a mental state of hopelessness and guilt, bringing a person to a cessation of activity called depression. In many cases, once again, sin is the problem because, "sin leads to guilt and depression, sinful handling further complicates matters lending a greater guilt and deeper depression, **ad infinitum**."[13]

Adams gives us three outlined steps that should be taken in order to help the depressed:

1. Counselors should check out complicating problems and set the counselee to work on dealing with these God's way. This should begin to lift the depression and reverse the spiral.

2. Next he should check out all factors and/or life patterns that may have led to the sinful reaction to the initial problem, urge and help the counselee to take biblical action in the power of the spirit to replace these patterns with biblical data.

---

[12]Ibid., 375.

[13]Ibid., 377.

3. The counselor must explain clearly the dynamics of depression to the counselee and set out for him/her a plan to attack sinful tendencies of the human heart that would surrender to feelings rather that follow the path of human responsibility.[14]

What Adams is seeking to establish is that depression can be dealt with. It is something that many Christians and non-Christians suffer from. Adams makes the stand that depression is many times from sin. But this many only stand to be true more so for unbelievers than for true believers. For example, if a mother lost her child at birth, this may cause severe depression. Other tragedies can happen in life that are way beyond our control to govern them. If something bad happens, it may not always be because of personal sin, in fact, it happen as a result of someone else's sin. We should encourage counselee's to seek God and trust at all time (even when bad things have happened to them for no apparent reason).

CHAPTER SUMMARY

It must be admitted that this short chapter does not due justice to the explanation of the full practice of nouthetic counseling. However, we will summarize what has been said here. First, we said that Christian counselor's must be fully aware that we are fighting a spiritual battle. The counselor is a soldier in the army of God seeking to equip the counselee to fight this battle. And, the counselor must have a good Biblical foundation.

---

[14]Ibid., 379.

Second, we discussed the fact that there is a sin problem. And sin must be dealt with and not covered over. Effective Christian Counselor's will speak the truth in love. Third, we discussed the fact that change is possible. We can't change the past, but, we can change our emotional responses to the present and future through forgiveness. Change is possible by the grace of God and the power of the Holy Spirit. Fourth, we discussed the importance of asking questions and gathering data. In order to effectively counsel, one must have all the background information before making any solid conclusion on a matter. Fifth, we talked about how to deal with anger. The improper ventilation of anger is unacceptable to God and must be treated as sin. People who "blow-up" hurt those people around them. Our emotions must be properly focused and channeled. We can learn to respond even as Jesus did: in love. Lastly, we learned that depression is a result of sin, or unpleasant events or happenings. One must learn to trust God at all times and realize that He is the one that governs our lives.

CHAPTER FIVE

CRISES COUNSELING

We live in a world in which crises seem to be taking place on many fronts, and as common occurrences. We can read in the daily newspaper, for example, and read about the tragedies that are taking place in our cities, states, and across the world. A crises can happen to anyone, at anyplace, and at anytime. A crises can bring an emotional stress to a person(s) that, would not normally be under stress in ordinary circumstances. Dr. H. Norman Wright says that,

a crises can be the result of one or more factors. It can be a problem that is too great or overwhelming, such as the death of a child. It could be a problem that to most people is not serious but for a given person has special significance and so becomes overwhelming for that individual. It could be a problem that comes at a time of special vulnerability or when the person is unprepared. Ordinarily people handle a stopped-up sink with no problem. But if it happens when they are sick, they may feel overwhelmed. It could occur when the person's normal coping mechanisms are not functioning well or when the person does not have support from others whom he or she needs.[1]

A crises can be a bad as the death of a loved one, or, it can be a simple as someone breaking a dish. If the person is at a vulnerable impasse, then, normal circumstances can turn into a crises situation as Wright has pointed out.

FOUR ELEMENTS OF A CRISES

I. A Hazardous event: "A hazardous event is some occurrence that starts a chain reaction of events culminating in a crises. A young wife who prepared for her career for seven years now discovers she is pregnant,"[2] for example.

II. The Vulnerable state: A person who is ill can become very intolerant of normal stress, especially if the person is sick with a life threatening illness (for an extended period of time). Also, a person who does not get much sleep at night for several days, will begin to be less tolerate to stress during the daytime.

III. The Precipitating factor: This level is "the straw that broke the Camel's back."[3] For example, some people may have experienced tremendous heartache and then fall apart over something like a broken dish. "These were the last straw, but the reaction

---

[1]H. Norman Wright, **Crises Counseling**, updated and ex. ed., (Ventura, Ca.: Regal Books, 1993), 20.

[2]Ibid., 21.

[3]Ibid., 21.

and tears are in response to the serious loss."[4]

IV.   The State of American Crises: "When a person can no longer handle a situation, the active crises develops."[5] Many people who reach this level experience depression, headaches, anxiety, or bleeding ulcers. They may also feel helpless, like there is no hope for the present or the future. These people tend to want immediate relief from the situation. Their normal responses to life can be reduced to 60% functioning level as well.

TRANSITION STAGES

Professionals in the field of counseling provide evidence that many people who go through major changes in life, such as a change in job, moving to a different state, or getting a divorce, will experience stress as a result. These rough transitional times are difficult to adjust to. Many people have retired into nothing and are bored to death. The Church has a great responsibility to help people through these adjustments and transition periods. Wright says that,

If we (the church) are going to lessen some of life's crises, we are to prepare our congregations in advance for the stages they will experience. This involves educating them to these stages of life and the actual transition they will go through, and helping them apply God's word so they are better able to.......

---

4 Ibid., 21.
5 Ibid., 21.

handle life's sudden changes as well as the predictable.[6]
The church should be a haven for all people, including people that
are in a crises situation. It is the church's responsibility to
take good care of people, especially the flock of God.

CRISES INTERVENTION

"Crises intervention is a way of providing immediate,
temporary, emotional first aid to victims of psychological and
physical trauma. The interviewer must react skillfully and quickly
to deal with behavior that is often disorganized, confused, and
potentially harmful."[7] It is important to understand that all
crises are different and will be handled differently in each
situation. "Some people tend to be optimistic, even in the midst
of crises; others are pessimistic and easily overwhelmed."[8]

The counselor should first attempt to calm the counselee down
and try to reduce the anxiety level. Collins says:

The counselor's calm, relaxed manner can help reduce anxiety
in the counselee, especially when this calmness is accompanied
by reassurance. Listen patiently and attentively as the
counselee describes the situation.[9]

---

[6]Ibid., 25.

[7]Collins, **Christian Counseling**, 65-66.

[8]Ibid., 66.

[9]Ibid., 67.

It is important that the counselor listen carefully to what has happened in the stressing situation, and that every attempt is made to calm the counselee down. Second, the counselor should help the client focus on the main issue at hand. The counselee should "try to focus on the present situation rather than discussing the past or pondering what might happen in the future."[10] Third, the counselor must instill hope in the life of the counselee in times of stress. Collins says,

> improvement is more likely if counselees can be given a sense of realistic hope about the future. Hope brings relief from suffering because it is based on a belief that things will get better. Hope helps us avoid despair and releases energy to meet the crises situation.[11]

Wright says that the counselor should "foster hope and positive expectations. Do not give them false promises, but encourage them to solve their problems. Your belief in their capabilities is important. This is a time when they need to borrow your hope and faith until theirs returns."[12] Fourth, the counselor must provide a support base for the counselee. The support base should be beyond just the counselor. It will reduce the demands on the counselor if the support base is expanded. Fifth, focused problem solving. This has been called the **backbone** of crises

---

[10]Ibid., 67.

[11]Ibid., 69.

[12]Wright, 84.

counseling. Wright says:

> You and the counselee try to determine the main problem that
> led to the crises, and then you help the person plan and
> implement ways to resolve it. You may discover other side
> issues and problems along the way, but you need to stay
> focused on this one problem until it is solved.[13]

DEPRESSION CRISES

Depression is called the "common cold" on mental disorders.[14]
It is more common now than ever before; furthermore, research
indicates that it disrupts the lives of 30-40 million people in the
USA. Depression is no respecter of persons, and history tells us
that many great leaders have suffered from it. In general, almost
all people have probably experienced some mild form of depression
after a personal disappointment or failure. However, "more severe
depression may overwhelm its victims with feeling of despair, fear,
exhaustion, immobilizing apathy, hopelessness, and inner
desperation."[15]

SIGNS OF DEPRESSION

There are at least seven major signs to look for in the
counselee that would be an indication that the person is
experiencing some form of depression (whether it is severe or

---

[13]Ibid., 89.

[14]Collins, 105.

[15]Ibid.

mild). (1) Sadness, along with pessimism and hopelessness; (2) apathy and inertia that make it difficult to get going in the morning; (3) a general fatigue; loss on energy and lack of interest in work, sex, religion, or hobbies; (4) low self-esteem, self-criticism and feelings of guilt, shame, worthlessness, and helplessness; (5) a loss in spontaneity; (6) insomnia and difficulties in concentration; and (7) loss of appetite.[16]

CAUSES OF DEPRESSION

First, it needs to be said that not all depression is caused by self-pity, or that it is wrong for a Christian to ever be depressed, or that depressed feeling could be removed permanently by spiritual excersizes (i.e., casting out Demons); or that happiness is a choice, or that a "depressed Christian is a contradiction in terms"[17] as some self-righteous right-wing fundamentalists have said. In reality, there are two major categories for causes of depression: (1) Genetic-biological causes; (2) the psychological-cognitive causes.[18]

The **genetic-biological** causes can stem from physical and/or chemical malfunctions in the body or brain. For example, thousands of women experience PMS, or post-partum depression after giving birth to a child. In addition to this, "other physical influences,

---

[16]Ibid.

[17]Ibid., 106.

[18]Ibid., 106-107.

like neurochemical malfunctioning, brain tumors, or glandular disorders, are more complicated creators of depression."[19] These, then, are some of the more common examples of genetic-biological causes of depression.

The **psychological-cognitive** causes can vary from age group. Studies show that the youth-culture experience a great deal more of depression. Collins states that "an estimated 25 percent of college students suffer from depression at one time, and 33 percent of college dropouts suffer from serious depression before leaving school."[20] Also, a person with a rotten family background may be more likely to become a depression victim, than say, someone with more healthy family environment. "Depression is more likely when parents blatantly or subtly reject their children or when status-seeking families set unrealistically high standards that children are unable to meet."[21]

The cognitive causes can stem from how the person **thinks** because, how a person thinks, will often enough determine how a person feels. If people think continually on the negative, then it is very likely that the person will go into a state of depression. It is factual to say, on the contrary, that positive people are the

---

[19]Ibid., 107.

[20]Ibid.

[21]Ibid., 108.

least likely to be depressed, simply because their whole outlook on life is better. People must learn to look at the positive side to things even in the face of difficult circumstances.

COUNSELING THE DEPRESSED

The minister or church worker can do much to help people who are struggling with depression. Depressed people tend to be isolated and therefore need to be reached out to. "Even social contacts or pastoral calls may be the starting point for counseling. Or perhaps a neighbor, friend or relative will ask you to make a contact because or his or her concern."[22] The depressed person needs to know that you really care about them, and want to help relieve their depression. The counselor should encourage the counselee to talk about the things in life that are bothering them. Counselors should "watch for talk about loses, failure, rejection, and other incidents that may have stimulated the current depression."[23]

A depressed person needs much reassurance. They need to be reassured again and again, in a warm and calm manner. The counselor should make every effort to keep the depressed person active and busy. Depressed people tend to be isolated and inactive, thinking too much, and therefore get more depressed. So, the counselor can set up specific plans of activity, such as a

---

[22]Wright, 110.

[23]Collins, 111.

detailed plan of activity with physical exercise as a part of the plan. Moderate forms of exercise can release hormones in the body that may help to lift the depression. There are hormones in the body that may help to lift the depression. For example, the hormone is called **catecholamine;** many runners experience a lift after their exercising. The point is that, *it is important to have the counselee get on a regular exercise schedule.*

If a person is suicidal, then, the person should be admitted to a hospital right away. Or, the other option is that they see a psychiatrist, because, the psychiatrist will be able to prescribe **anti-depressant medication** to help with the depression. If they are admitted, the counselee should remain hospitalized until the medication is taking effect and the person has received counseling.

The sad truth is that there is no hard evidence that depression can be completely prevented. Especially if the causes are **genetic-biological** in nature. However, helping the depressed counselee to learn to trust God is a good start. "A conviction that God is alive and in control can give hope and encouragement, even when we are inclined to be discouraged and without hope."[24] Hope is available because we serve a God of hope who cares deeply for us. Once the depressed person believes this truth, then, there will be a great change in their whole outlook on life. Many times, a simple new relationship with someone from the church, who is reaching out to those that are suffering, can suffice and carry one to that next new season of renewed hope for the future. **As the church operates in the force of love, people will respond in a positive manner, especially, for those in psychological need.**

---

24 Ibid., 115.

CHAPTER SUMMARY

It was necessary to cover "crises counseling" in this paper because, many people are or have experienced some sort crises situation. These crises will come and go, and will vary in length of time. We said that crises will in many cases come to those people who are not prepared to deal with transitional phases of life such as, divorce, a new job, moving out of state, and retirement. We also said that crises intervention should provide immediate/temporary relief by calming the person down, thereby, reducing the stress and anxiety level. The counselor must instill hope for the future to the person who is in the crises; get them to stay focused on the true problem in the present. Lastly, we said that depression is more common that ever before. It is a major cause of suicide and must be addressed. We listed several signs of depression, looked to the two major cause (i.e., genetic-biological and psychological-cognitive); and we briefly talked about how to counsel the depressed.

CHAPTER SIX

MARRIAGE COUNSELING

The USA is suffering from a terrible crises of marital
breakdowns. It is now easily estimated that one out of every two
marriages ends, tragically, in divorce. One author states that,

> at a typical counseling center, half of those coming for
> counseling come primarily because of marital conflicts and
> another one-quarter come because of marital-related conflicts.
> It is estimated that over 20 million couples in the United
> States are unhappy and unfulfilled.[1]

The statistics for divorce and marital problems are staggering.
Moreover, it is clear that there are some deep-rooted sin problems
that have crept into many Christian marriages. There is a great need
for pastors and church leaders to practice marriage counseling.
"Evangelical pastoral counselors do most of the premarital counseling
in America today and in addition often help couples through what they
say in the pulpit."[2]

---

1 Paul D. Meier et al., **Introduction to Psychology and Counseling**,
  333.
2 Ibid., 333.

PULPIT COUNSELING

Many troubled marriages could be helped through the ministry of pastor-teacher. It is up to the pastor to lay foundations for the Christian life. Such concepts as serving, faithfulness, living a responsible Christian life, regular church attendance, and a firm commitment to the word of God as final authority in the life of a believer.

The word of God should be preached with passion. The pastor needs to have a firm conviction that most of peoples problems can be solved by the word of God, and prayer. If the word of God is not the chief aim in the pulpit, then, the pastor should expect to see his office full of counselee's. Contrariwise, there will be good results of preaching the word of God in the pulpit; a good Bible based pulpit ministry is essential to helping people deal with life and its difficulties. Many pastors say that the people who come in for counseling the most, are the same people who have poor devotional habits, such as, regular Bible study, prayer, and good Christian fellowship. It could generally be said that, most Christians who have a growing relationship to the Lord, are doing pretty good in their marriage. As our vertical relationship with God is in order, then, our horizontal relationships will be good too.

GOALS AND ROLES OF MARRIAGE COUNSELING

The first goal is counseling, is that we want the couple to

resolve their problems in a Biblical manner with Biblical guidance. In general, however, there are five basic goals that marriage counselors should seek to achieve: (1) Help the couple to solve interpersonal conflicts, and help them to improve their communication with each other; (2) encourage each partner to meet the emotional needs and sexual needs of their spouse; (3) help to clarify marriage roles and responsibilities; (4) help build Christian values in the family by turning to the word of God for Biblical answers; and (5) teach the couple how to handle stress effectively.[3]

The counselor should have a solid understanding of his/her role in the counseling setting. The counselor is to listen to the and gather all the information about the problem so that the problems can be accurately assessed. Essentially, there are seven things that they marriage counselor should seek to do:

1. The counselor should help stimulate healthy interaction.

2. They should function as observers.

3. They should participate in family interactions.

4. They should seek to temper the destructive features of conflicts.

5. They should help the counselee's to take responsibility, and challenge denials.

6. They will function as educators.

---

[3]Ibid., 335.

7. They will, or should be, fine examples of mental health.[4] The counselor, then, will have several goals in mind as the counselee's and the counselor meet together. Having established clear-cut goals will help the couple progress towards a directed end in mind. And, the counselor will do a much better job in the whole process if the goals are kept in mind.

The major goal in marriage counseling should be to help the couple have their lives conform to the image of Jesus Christ. They (the couple) will need to learn how to listen to one another, recognize truth in what the other person is saying, meet one anothers needs, and build their lives upon the unchanging truths and principles of God's word.

INFIDELITY

One of the clearest reasons for unfaithfulness or infidelity is the fact that emotional and sexual needs are not being met in the marriage itself. The most basic needs for men are: (1) Sexual fulfillment; (2) recreational companionship; (3) an attractive spouse; (4) domestic support; and (5) admiration.[5] It is interesting to note that many men have fallen into adultery because their number one need of sex is not being met. Women, on the other

---

[4]Ibid., 335.

[5]H. Norman Wright, **Marriage Counseling**, updated and expanded, (Ventura, Ca.: Regal Books, 1995), 158.

hand, have a somewhat different set of needs: (1) Affection; (2) conversation; (3) honesty and openness; (4) financial support; and (5) family commitment.[6] The counselor needs to be aware that these are the most basic needs of men and women and will need to ask probing questions to find out which needs are not being met.

CAUSES FOR MARITAL PROBLEMS

It should be remembered that marital conflict often is a symptom of something deeper, such as selfishness, lack of love, unwillingness to forgive, anger, bitterness, communication problems, anxiety, sexual abuse, drunkenness, feelings of inferiority, sin, and a deliberate rejection of God's will.[7]

All of these causes of marital problems are indirectly and directly mentioned in the Bible. One of the greatest keys to marital success is found in Luke 9:23 where Jesus says: "If anyone wishes to be my disciple, he must pick up his cross daily and follow me." The cross is the main cure-all for the selfishness in peoples lives. People who deliberately reject God's will, in the end, will not submit to any human authority. **Men and women who want to remain autonomous will not be likely candidates for a successful marriage.** We must teach people to serve others, to serve their spouses, to seek their needs only after they have sought to meet

---

[6]Ibid., 159.

[7]Collins, **Christian Counseling**, 409.

the needs of their mate. The causes of marital problems, however, are not always related to sin or selfishness, there could be a host of other reasons. People could have great pressure from their jobs, financial struggles, personality conflicts, etc. For a further discussion about possible causes of marital conflicts and how to deal with them, consult Gary Collins book entitled, **Christian Counseling: A Comprehensive Guide**, pp. 409-413.

FOUR PRINCIPLES FOR PREVENTING MARITAL PROBLEMS

I. **Teach Biblical principles of marriage.** There are guidelines and principles in Scripture that need to be followed in order to have a successful marriage. Collins says: "We live in a society that propagates non-biblical views about sex and marriage, so the biblical teaching about sex and the meaning of love need to be reinforced frequently."[8]

II. **Stress the importance of marriage, marriage enrichment, and marital commitment.** We live in a culture that pulls us away from the family structure and the time that it takes to build a great marriage. Again, Collins says that "marriage takes time, effort, and commitment if it is to grow and develop. This needs to be emphasized in churches and elsewhere. Encourage people to make marriage a high priority item in terms of expenditure of time and

---

[8]Ibid., 420.

effort...Help them establish priorities, work toward mutual goals, and think of ways to bring variety into their marriages."[9]

III. **Teach principles of communication and conflict resolution.** Married people will need to be "shown the importance of listening, self-disclosure, mutual acceptance, and understanding. Empathy, warmth, and genuineness do not need to be limited to counseling sessions. These attributes can be learned and practiced in marriage and throughout the church."[10]

IV. **Encourage counseling when needed.** Many people are reluctant or embarrassed about the need for counseling. Therefore, it can be encouraged from the pulpit that it is a sign of great strength to seek counseling. Encourage people to seek counseling early before the problems get progressively worse.[11]

---

[9]Ibid., 420-421.

[10]Ibid., 412.

[11]Ibid.

CHAPTER SEVEN

PSYCHOTHERAPY AND COUNSELING

INTRODUCTION

Psychology is the study of the human **psyche**, the study of the mind. Psychology also deals with the individual person and covers all aspects of human behaviors related to the psyche. Psychotherapy and counseling, on the other hand, is the art of helping other people overcome their personal problems. Moreover, it is helping them grow in mental, emotional, and spiritual health. Psychotherapy seeks to develop the wholeness of the individual person. Therapy seeks to make permanent changes in the individual, whereas counseling is geared toward giving people advice.

DEFINITION

The term "psychotherapy" may be used to describe the process of helping people with severe problems. "Psychotic disorders and other major psychological problems require intensive treatment by professionals who have spent many years learning to deal specifically with these problems."[1] Another definition by Everett L. Worthington states that,

Psychotherapy is generally systematic helping that intends to

---

[1]Paul D. Meier et al, **Introduction to Psychology and Counseling**, 297.

assist the client deal with problems in living that are extremely bothersome or that interfere with the person's ability to function personally, socially, or occupationally. Psychotherapy is generally concerned with psychopathology, assess clients or patients using formal diagnosis, and attempts to make long-term personality changes more frequently than do other forms of counseling. Psychotherapy may include individual therapy, group therapy, marital therapy, or family therapy.[2]

THREE TYPES OF COUNSELING OR THERAPY

There are three main types of counseling and therapy: outpatient psychotherapy or counseling, psychiatric inpatient treatment, and community counseling.

OUTPATIENT COUNSELING OR PSYCHOTHERAPY

This type deals with people who need either individual therapy, group therapy, marital therapy, or family therapy. These people have serious problems, needless to say. But their problems are not so serious as to need to go to the psychiatric ward in a mental hospital. What we are dealing with at this level is counseling people deal with problems that have produced emotional distress, interpersonal tensions, or other disruptions in normal living. This level of counseling deals with people who need others

---

[2]Everett L. Worthington, Jr., ed., **Psychotherapy and Religious Values,** (Grand Rapids, Mi.: Baker Book House, 1993), 29.

to help the overcome their difficult circumstances. In many cases, pastoral counseling will help Christians at this level.

PSYCHIATRIC INPATIENT TREATMENT

These are clinics that have been established that will provide total psychiatric care of people "who are unable to function as outpatients or people who desire total immersion in a psychiatric community to speed recovery from serious psychological difficulties."[3] Treatment will include daily contact with a counselor or psychotherapist, or regular visits from a Psychiatrist, and a good dose of group therapy. There will be other activities such as sports, Bible study and prayer, school, and other recreational activities.[4]

COMMUNITY COUNSELING

Everrett L. Worthington, Jr., says that community counseling involves "an array of preventive, psycho-educational, and counseling interventions that seek to prevent mental health problems, promote positive mental health, and treat mental health problems within the resources of the community. With that definition, pastoral activities such as sermons, premarital counseling, educational groups, and even discipleship or Bible-study groups might be legitimately considered community

---

[3]Ibid., 30.

[4]Ibid., 30-31.

counseling.[5]

SPECIFIC METHODS OF PSYCHOTHERAPY AND COUNSELING

It should be said here that, many secular methods of therapy have worked in helping people recover from their problems. However, not all methods and practices are neither Biblical or completely effective in helping people recover from their problems. The goal in this section is to give an overview of some of the methods and make a few comments about the positive and the negative things about the methods of psychotherapy.

PSYCHOANALYSIS

This is the oldest systematic method for treating people with psychological problems. Sigmond Freud (1859-1939) is the founder of which most modern psychoanalytic theory derives its work from. The goal is to solve the inner struggle between the super-ego (i.e., the conscience) and the id (i.e., the natural drives of man). He attempted to do this by developing a method called "free-association." The patient lays on the couch in a relaxed state. "The patient is asked to talk about whatever he or she wishes, including memories and feelings. The therapist then asks the patient for thoughts, fantasies, and feelings associated with material given."[6] As the therapist and the patient talk, the therapist helps the patient accept themselves and work through

---

[5]Ibid., 31.

[6]Meier et al, 301.

their deepest inner conflicts. Meier explains:

> Psychoanalytic theory states that as patients "experience" acceptance from the analyst, they accept and "love" themselves more, and hence, with growing self-tolerance, their defenses against subconscious conflict diminish.[7]

As Christians we must recognize that this is only a partial solution, at best. Jesus Christ is the real answer to the inner conflicts that people struggle with. Through forgiveness of sin and inner healing by the power of the Holy Spirit, the inner conflicts get quickly resolved.

BEHAVIOR MODIFICATION

In essence, behavior therapy seeks to bring changes in overt behavior(s). "Direct behavior modifications leads to changes in feelings and attitudes. The therapist expects clients to set specific goals to aid in their own treatment. Behavior modification works particularly well with phobias and obsessive thinking."[8] For example, sometimes alcoholics will be punished by mild electric shocks when they go on a drinking binge. The reason for this, is that, the patient will develop a **phobia** to the smell or taste of alcohol, and therefore avoid alcohol altogether. In other cases, the therapist will develop a written contract between themselves and the patient. For example, a person may do this who

---

[7]Ibid., 301.

[8]Ibid., 304.

wants to stop smoking cigarettes. And when the person starts to smoke less, then, they receive some sort of a reward for their behavior changes and modification, and so on.

although the behavior modification therapy has its strong points, it has its weaknesses too. As Christians, we must understand that true character change happens as a result of the work of the Holy Spirit. We are not saying that people do not genuinely get helped by this method of therapy, what we are saying is that the Christian counselor must put the emphasis of the individuals walk with God, repentance from sin, and fear of the Lord. Many Christians have addictions like this, for the simple reason that they have lost their fear of the Lord.

RATIONAL-EMOTIVE THERAPY (RET)

This type of therapy was developed by Albert Ellis, and is "an extension of behaviorism that emphasizes the influence of beliefs upon behavior...These irrational beliefs must be located, confronted, and then replaced by more rational beliefs."[9] Meier explains the goal and nature of RET by saying:

The goal of therapy is to minimize a self-defeating outlook and help an individual acquire a more realistic, total philosophy of life. Pain may be alleviated in several ways, including diversion, satisfaction of demands, and convincing a person to give up demandingness. Counselees are taught

[9]Ibid., 306.

62

basically how to think-to separate the rational from the irrational beliefs.

The rational-emotive therapist is informal, active, energetic, and directive. Often a forceful approach is necessary to alter destructive patterns of behavior. Homework assignments and facing unpleasant events are part of the therapy.[10] Essentially, the patients need to be shown that they are resistant to changing their negative outlook or behavior because, change is hard and they would prefer simple or instantaneous solutions that are not feasible.

CLIENT-CENTERED THERAPY

This is known as the Rogerian method of psychotherapy. Rogers believed that people need to regain contact with their feelings and personal values. The therapist will listen to the patient and let the patient talk about their problems. The client should be able to solve their problems by talking things out thereby recognizing what the problem is (so the theory goes). The patient will experience acceptance and affirmation which will help the patient get free. The problem with this method is that, in many cases, people are so confused that they are unable to recognize or see the problem (which could be in them). This theory assumes the innate goodness of man. The fact is that man has not been able to recognize his problems from the beginning. Therefore, we believe

_____

[10]Ibid., 307.

that there is not much value in this method in terms of admitting that people can solve their own problems simply by talking to someone and being able to recognize it. For a greater detailed critique of this therapy, you can consult Jay E. Adams book entitled **Competent to Counsel**, (Grand Rapids, Mi.: Zondervans, 1970), 78-104.

GESTALT THERAPY

This method seeks to create experiences that will increase the individuals self-awareness. "When individuals know and accept themselves to the fullest extent possible, they can overcome conflicts within their personalities so that psychological growth occurs."[11]

REALITY THERAPY

This therapy seeks to get the patient to focus on behaving responsibly. The three R's must be observed to do this: face reality, do right, and be responsible. The focus is on the present rather than on past feelings or experiences. Meier says:

Individuals must face reality and admit that the past cannot be rewritten. They must accept full responsibility for the present and future behavior. Unconscious motivations are no excuse for misbehavior...The therapist helps individuals devise specific plans for their behavior and make a commitment

---

[11]Ibid., 308.

to follow through with those plans.[12]

The strength of this method and philosophy is that, there is a strong emphasis and focus on personal responsibility for one's self and actions. In fact, **reality therapy** has had the greatest impact on Christian Counseling. However, the weakness of the therapy is that *"reality therapy morality is relative because it is based on no absolute standards."*[13]

ALDERIAN PSYCHOTHERAPY

Alfred Alder (1927) was the founder of this philosophy of therapy. He did not believe people could be mentally ill; rather, **he believed that people were discouraged because of self-defeating inferiority complexes.**[14] Alder believed that human beings were creative people with **self-determined destinies.** People create the meaning of their life by goals set and finding personal meaning by pursuing them. The positive side of this type of therapy is that people need to focus on goals and personal fulfillment. The weakness is that it is entirely **humanistic,** in that, you can find ultimate meaning and purpose apart from fulfilling a *God-given destiny.*

---

12 Ibid., 309.
13 Ibid.
14 Ibid.

LOGOTHERAPY

Victor Frankl is the founder of logotherapy. He wanted to get people to focus on what gives life meaning. Life is meaningful when our spiritual nature is then satisfied. Logotherapy, then, is helping the patient find true meaning in life. The Christian counselor will point to Christ as the answer to life, and Christ will give the person true meaning. This therapy has much to commend it.

INTEGRITY THERAPY

O. Hobert Mower developed integrity therapy. He believed that people feel guilty because of sin in their life. Therefore, the solution for sin and emotional problems, is for the clients to recognize their sin, confess it, and forsake it. They should ask Christ for forgiveness and make restitution if necessary. Integrity therapy is most compatible with nouthetic counseling. Nouthetic counseling and its techniques combine integrity therapy and elements of behavioral psychology. This therapy is the closest method to Christianity solution to man's problems. It is Biblically based and has much to commend it.

PHYSICAL INTERVENTIONS

In addition to verbal counseling, Psychiatrists treat certain physical problems by medical means. This includes, but not limited to, the use of medication, shock therapy, and psychosurgery.

PSYCHOACTIVE DRUGS

One of the most effective treatments for depression has come from drugs such as, but not limited to, Elavil, Trofanil, Norpramine, Lithium salt, Tranquilizers, Thorazine, Haldol, and others have helped both manic-depressives and schizophrenics. In many cases, drugs and counseling will bring normality in a persons life.

ELECTRIC SHOCK TREATMENT

This is called ECT for Electroconvulsive therapy. It was introduced in 1938 for people who were psychotic or who had extreme emotional and mental disorders. But, since the 1950's, it is not used that much since we now have so many effective psychoactive drugs. Meier says that,

> ECT is sometimes used for suicidal crises because anti-depressants do not take effect for a period of two or three weeks. Usually 5 to 8 treatments are given for depressive disorders. Following a course of ECT, 30 to 40 percent of the patients will relapse within a year because the root psychological and spiritual causes of the depression were not uncovered and resolved.[15]

Today ECT is not used, unless, the person is suffering from severe depression, and, all other forms or therapy have failed. Also, there is a bad side effect of short-term memory loss in the patients as a result of ECT.

---

[15]Ibid., 312.

PSYCHOSURGERY

The use of surgery on the brain was introduced by Egas Moniz (1935). Prefrontal lobotomy is the cutting of the frontal lobe of the brain to make people more compliant and relieve their emotional pain. Surgery is also used to treat lesions in the temporal lobe of the brain that cause changes in normal behavior.

CHAPTER EIGHT

CHRISTIAN PSYCHIATRY

The purpose of this chapter is to examine the nature of Christian psychiatry, and how it relates to helping the Christian counselor. There are many ultra-conservatives who say that there is no such thing as "Christian" psychiatry. However, we believe that there is such a thing.

DEFINITION OF CHRISTIAN PSYCHIATRY

Dr. Frank B. Minirth, M.D., and Dr. Walter Byrd, M.D., define Christian Psychiatry by saying:

In Christian Psychiatry the counselor is concerned not only with psychological and physical problems, but also with spiritual problems, whereas in other approaches to counseling, sometimes the spiritual aspect of man is, unfortunately, not addressed. In Christian Psychiatry the counselor is concerned with understanding the Psychological make-up of man and how psychodynamic factors have implanted on each individual's function. In Christian Psychiatry the counselor is aware that physical problems may be contributing to an apparent spiritual or psychological problem. In other words, a balanced Christian counseling approach should deal with the whole of man.[1]

Essentially, then, Christian Psychiatry is a wholistic approach to helping people with problems. Unlike secular psychology and psychiatry, Christian Psychiatry takes the spiritual nature of man into account as a source, but not necessarily the primary one, of an individuals problems.

In many cases, people have, ultimately, spiritual problems. They feel guilty because, they are guilty. They feel lonely because, in many cases, they are sperate from God because of sin. It is the role of the Christian Counselor, therefore, to look at and examine a clients walk with God.

A THEOLOGY OF CHRISTIAN PSYCHIATRY

Many people have been damaged emotionally and psychologically because, they were raised in a strict-legalistic-religious home. Many ultra-conservatives have focused on the law and good works as a means of personal salvation. It is essential to understand the grace of God: his unmerited favor. There is nothing we can do to earn this grace. Understanding the doctrine of grace is necessary in Christian counseling. Otherwise, we will not be able to help people who have felt condemned by God all their lives because they failed to live up to His holiness and standards. Minirith says:

Grace implies that the love of God is free and unmerited.

---

[1]Frank B. Minirith, M.D., and Walter Byrd, M.D., **Christian Psychiatry**, rev. and ex. ed., (Grand Rapids, Mi.: Fleming H. Revell, 1990), 11.

70

Just as parents accept their children and will have an innate love for them regardless of what they do, so God loves us.[2] Parents, therefore, must never reject their children no matter what sin they may commit or fall into. This does not mean, then, that they are to approve of their ill behavior; but our children must always know that we love them. Research shows that "Christians may become discouraged, neurotic, or even psychotic if they feel their receiving or keeping Christ is conditional."[3]

The message of works-righteousness and legalism is the opposite of the grace of God. It says that Christ will accept you "if" you keep all the rules and regulations. The doctrine of grace relates to the practice of Christian psychiatry because, the patients must feel that same love and acceptance from the psychiatrist or Christian counselor. The counselor, however, does not accept irresponsible behavior, but, an "understanding of grace is foundational to Christian psychiatry as well as to the Bible."[4]

THE THREE PART NATURE OF MAN

The three-fold nature of man has long been recognized by theologians. Some scholars have debated as to whether the spirit and soul of man is one, or is separate. But what is important is not whether the trichotomy or dichotomy view is correct, but simply

---

[2]Ibid., 34.

[3]Ibid., 35.

[4]Ibid., 46.

71

to recognize that man has three essential elements: spiritual, soul (i.e., the mind, will, and emotions), and a body. And these are the three elements of man's nature that Christian psychiatry deals with.

We need to understand the people can have a variety of problems that can be emotional, spiritual, mental and psychological, or organic in nature. In Christian counseling, it is often discovered that there is a conflict between the conscience of man and his basic drives, or sinful nature. In secular language, this is called the conflict between the super-ego and the id. But in reality, in many cases, clients may be experiencing conflict between their carnal nature and the Holy Spirit. Not that there is a struggle in man with two equal-opposite natures, but that there is a struggle with the flesh or sinful nature in man. The client will have to grow in his or her relationship with Christ, and trust the Holy Spirit to help them overcome the fleshy conflicts.

The soul is made up of the mind, the will, and emotions. The reason that many Christian still struggle with sin, or have difficulties is that they have not had their minds renewed by the word of God. The spirit of man gets saved, by the soul is being renewed day-by-day (Romans 12:1). We believe that as people grow in Christ, many, if not all, of people's emotional problems will go away.

Also, in Christian psychiatry, the doctors are able to prescribe drugs and medication to patients who need them. In many cases the drugs are prescribed for people with severe depression problems. In many cases, people will have a chemical imbalance in their brain that cause manic behavior, depression, and psychotic episodes to occur. Once these patients are stable, then, we can proceed with Christian counseling and attempt to treat the spiritual side of man.

Christian psychiatry is a wholistic approach to treating people with problems. It attempts to treat man spiritually, physically, and in the realm of the soul. Again, the difference between secular psychiatry and Christian psychiatry, is that the former fails to recognize the spiritual nature of man and treat it, while the latter takes into account the fact that man is spiritual, and that the spiritual side of man must be treated. This can only be done by restoring man's relationship to God through Jesus Christ. This, then, is the primary value of Christian psychiatry.

CHAPTER NINE

CONCLUSION

We have seen is this paper that there is a great need for
Christian counseling in today's complicated world. Moreover,
people need help in solving their problems. This is the job of the
Christian counselor in particular. They are to help people solve
problems in all three areas of their life: Spirit, soul, and body.

Man lives is a world where knowledge is increasing at a
phenomenal rate. Our society is very confused and, the family
structure has broken down. As a result of this breakdown, the need
for Christian counseling has risen to a higher level than in the
past. In many cases, however, secular psychology and counseling
have failed to deal with the main problem of man: that he is a
spiritual being and, man needs to be restored and reconciled in his
relationship with his creator. If this fact is ignored by the
Christian counselor, then, he or she has failed in their role as a
"Christian counselor" in helping people.

I am not saying that people outside of Christ cannot be helped
at all; but, what I am saying is that secular methods and
psychotherapy does not, nor can it, change the sinful nature of
man. Mankind does not need external reformation, rather, he is in

need of internal transformation. This, in fact, will change his sinful nature thereby changing his or her bad behavior. For truly that is what psychology and psychotherapy seeks to do. But it can't without Christ.

Christian psychology, psychiatry, and counseling will fail, unless, they are pointing people to Jesus Christ as the key foundation of their life. As we discussed in chapter three on Nouthetic Counseling, this is the goal.

The foundation, then, for successful Christian counseling, is the word of God and the guidance of the Holy Spirit. All other methods, tools, techniques, etc., are only aids in helping the patient to recover and get help. The greatest help is to lead someone to Christ as Lord and savior. If the Christian counselor can do this, then, they have accomplished much to truly help someone.

APPENDIX ONE

HOW TO COUNSEL THE HOMOSEXUAL

We have an epidemic proportion of people who are "coming out of the closet" with their sexual preferences. It is important to understand that many people struggle with homosexuality. It is very unfortunate that many little boys and girls have suffered from sexual abuse that have later on in life caused many problems in their personal lives.

Homosexuals and lesbians need to understand the difference between God's hatred for their sin and, His love and compassion for them. Many right-wing groups, for example, have sent out the wrong message to the homosexual and lesbian community. It is typical of both groups to feel that "if" there is a God up there, that they are sure that He hates them. It is unfortunate that many groups have communicated a God of hate and wrath to the homosexual community. Thus, further isolating them for the real Christian God and message.

Homosexuals and lesbians need to realize that Jesus died for them. No one is excluded from the message of the gospel based on their sexual sins. Indeed, these sins can be forgiven. I believe that if Jesus were walking on the earth today, that, he would not be afraid of hanging out with them. He would not treat them like lepers that need to be quarantined like many Christian groups have.

The message that we need to send out is one of hope. Our job is to minister the word of God to them. God loves them, yet, He hates sin because He is Holy. It is true that homosexuality is one of the most vial and decadent sins, but it can be forgiven. The Christian counselor needs to let the homosexual know that God will forgive them and, that He deeply cares for them. Granted they must be first willing to repent of their wicked ways. God can and will change their perverted nature. Thousands of ex-homosexuals can testify to this fact.

As people understand God's heart toward them, then they will not be so turned-off to the Christian community. It is true that most homosexuals know already that they are filthy-dirty-sinners and, they know down deep inside that there is a God. Therefore, the message of the Christian counselor toward the homosexual will not be one of wrath and judgment, rather it will be that, it is the lovingkindness of God that will lead them to repentance.

APPENDIX TWO

THE PROBLEM WITH MODERN PSYCHOLOGY: WHY IT DOESN'T WORK

Why is it that modern psychology doesn't change people? I believe that the answer lies in the presuppositions of secular psychology. That is that, secular psychology believes or says that the answer lies within yourself. Most of the time people are taught or counseled to focus on themselves.

Some call psychology "the cult of self-worship" as we saw in chapter two. But this is the precise nature of our problem: we are innately selfish people. To tell a self-centered person that they answer is within themselves is absurdity. The more people are indoctrinated with selfishness, the worse they will get. The central reason that this "self-help" message is wrong and, that it doesn't work, is that, it is the antithesis of Jesus' message. Jesus said, in fact, that we must deny ourselves (e.g., Luke 9:23). The answer that secular psychology gives is analogous to counseling a 300 pound overweight person to eat more greasy hamburgers as the answer to their weight problems. We all know that this is absurd; yet, this is exactly what this "self" philosophy is doing. It only fuels the problem. This entire message is completely contrary to the clear teaching of Jesus in the New Testament.

Again, the main reason why secular psychology does not work (meaning that it does not change peoples sinful nature), is because its salvation message is to focus on self (which is the main problem). Self is not the answer: Jesus is. Serving Jesus is the what we should focus on. And, as we seek our identity in Him life will be meaningful and fulfilling. We were created to give and to serve other people, not to be self-absorbing, that only brings death and suffocation. This is why psychology as such is totally bankrupt and, has no real life-changing solutions. It only provides temporary band-aids that cover the real problem: self.

APPENDIX THREE

DEMON POSSESSION: THE DEVIL MADE ME DO IT SYNDROME

"The Devil made me do it" one teenager once told me. What the young boy was really saying is that it was not his fault for his immoral behavior, it was the Devil who made him sleep with his girl-friend. The fact is that we cannot blame the Devil or anyone else, for that matter, on our bad behavior. We are responsible for our sins and actions. Even truly Demon possessed people who kill, rob, and rape, will go to prison if they get caught. My point is that Christians need to stop blaming the demons for their sins and problems.

When a person commits adultery, beats his wife, swears at his boss, etc., it is not because of the Devil or his demons. It is because of his own personal sin. Sure people get tempted by Satan to do this or that, but ultimately we are the ones who will decide whether or not we will commit the act. I have been in ministries where the minister is trying to cast this or that person out of a believer (who can only be oppressed, not possessed) to get this person delivered from lust or masturbation, for example. Most of the time, it is the flesh that is not under the control of the Holy Spirit that is the cause of the problem. A true believer can only be oppressed and not Demon possessed.

I believe that it is time for many Christians to start taking personal responsibility for their sin. Pentecostals and Charismatics need to stop blaming the Devil for personal sin. People sin because they want to, not because the Devil made them do anything.

SELECTED BIBLIOGRAPHY

Adams, Jay E. **Competent to Counsel: Introduction to Nouthetic Counseling.** Grand Rapids, Mi.: Zondervans, 1970.

_____. **The Christian Counselor's Manual: The Practice of Nouthetic Counseling.** Grand Rapids, Mi.: Zondervans, 1970.

Collins, Ph.D., Gary R. **Christian Counseling: A Comprehensive Guide.** Dallas, Tx.: Word Publishing, 1988.

_____. **Case Studies in Christian Counseling.** Dallas, Tx.: Word Publishing, 1991.

Johnston, J. Kirk. **When Counseling is not Enough: Biblical Answers for those who still struggle.** Grand Rapids, Mi.: Discovery House, 1994.

Meier, M.D., Paul D. et al. **Introduction to Psychology and Counseling.** 2nd ed. Grand Rapids, Mi.: Baker Book House, 1991.

Minirith, M.D., Frank B. and Walter Byrd, M.D. **Christian Psychiatry.** rev. and ex. ed. Grand Rapids, Mi.: Fleming H. Revell, 1990.

Narramore, Clyde M. **The Psychology of Counseling.** Grand Rapids, Mi.: Zondervans, 1960.

Owen, Jim. **Christian Psychology's War on God's Word: The Victimization of the Believer.** Santa Barbara, Ca.: Eastgate, 1993.

Vitz, Paul C. **Psychology as Religion: The Cult of Self-Worship.** 2nd ed. Grand Rapids, Mi.: Wm B. Eerdmans, 1977.

White, John. **Putting the Soul Back in Psychology.** Illinois: Intervarsity Press, 1987.

Worthington, Jr., Everett L. **Psychotherapy and Religious Values.**
Grand Rapids, Mi.: Baker Book House, 1993.

Wright, H. Norman. **Crises Counseling.** updated and ex. ed.
Ventura, Ca.: Regal Books, 1995.

_____. **Marriage Counseling.** updated and ex. ed. Ventura, Ca.:
Regal Books, 1995.

About The Author

Dr. Craig Lantz has been an ordained minister for over 20 years, he has ministry experience in college and youth ministry, and has been involved in several mission outreaches overseas to Europe in Ireland, Germany, England, Holland, and Norway, as well as outreaches in South America to the Capital of Brazil, Rio De Janerio.

Dr. Lantz graduated from Western Michigan University in 1986, with a Bachelor's of Science degree. While attending WMU he became very involved in student ministry, campus evangelism, and desired to serve the Lord Jesus Christ on a full-time basis ministering primarily to college and university students.

In 1991, Dr. Lantz enrolled in Covington Theological Seminary, Rossville, Georgia. He earned the Master of Ministry degree, and then went on to study theology and earned the Master of Theology degree. From there, he still felt such a hunger for God's word, he enrolled in a Master of Arts degree in Biblical Studies where every book of the Old and New Testaments were studied in detail. He graduated from Trinity Theological Seminary with a Master of Arts degree in Biblical Studies in the summer of 1994.

Although Dr. Lantz loved the study of *theology* (which is from the Greek word, *theos*, or God, so theology meaning, the study of God), he found that his biggest delight was in the study of the Scriptures themselves. He is fascinated with the Old Testament Panorama from Genesis all the way to Malachi, the last Old Testament prophet. He received his Doctor of Philosophy degree (PhD) in Religious Studies from International Seminary in 1998.

Books by Craig Lantz

Available to order at Amazon.com

A Biblical Survey of the Old Testament:
A Brief and Concise Guide to Understanding the Old Testament

A Biblical Survey of the New Testament:
A Concise Handbook on the New Testament Canonical Books

Christian Counseling: An Introduction
A Concise Guide for Ministers and Christian Workers in the Field of Christian Counseling

CHURCH LAW:
A Concise Legal Handbook for Ministers, Pastors, and Church Leaders

Ethics:
A Concise Handbook on Contemporary Issues

Hermeneutics: The Science and Art of Biblical Interpretation
A Brief and Concise Handbook on How to Interpret the Bible

Philosophy of Religion:
An Examination of the Arguments for the Existence of God, and the Problem of Evil

Systematic Theology:
A Brief and Concise Handbook

The Role of Faith and Grace in the Life and Theology of Dietrich Bonhoeffer:
Pastor, Theologian, Prophet, and Martyr

World Religions: An Investigation of the Origins, Nature, and Doctrines of Seven Major World Religions
A Brief and Concise Handbook on Seven non-Christian Religions

www.ingramcontent.com/pod-product-compliance
Lightning Source LLC
Chambersburg PA
CBHW051947280526

45789CB00009B/3204